Tina
Unexpected Pleasure, Unanticipated Pain

Author Desiree L Woods

Illustrators: Jonathan Kimbel
               Roshanay Fatima

To Help Bridge the Gap in Relations and Provide Support

TINA
Unexpected Pleasure, Unanticipated Pain©
Copyright 2024

All rights reserved. This book or parts thereof,
May not be reproduced in any form without permission with
The exception in the case of brief quotations embodied in critical
article and reviews for promotion.

For information address:
Desiree L Woods
Daymart Textile Services & Outlet, LLC
2785 East Grand Boulevard, Detroit, MI 48202
daymart.services@gmail.com

INDEX

About the Author

Dedication Page

Preface

Famous Teen Moms

Introduction

Abstraction

Hindsight

The Objective of This Book

In Memory of Those That Moved to Heaven

Overcoming Stares and Comments

To The Family

Don't Give Up on Your Dreams

Unexpected Pleasures-Unanticipated Pain

Win Some, Lose Some – Friends

INDEX

Family – Overcoming What People Say

Trusting the Process

Overturned - for those who come from toxic environments

Positive Affirmations

Abstractions—Poetic Writings –

I suppose I'll have a Baby

I Forgive You Mother

Services for Teen Moms

Teen Parent connections

Housing for Teen Moms

Resources for Teen Moms

Counseling for Teen Moms

Resources for Teen Moms

Employment For Younger Teens

ABOUT THE AUTHOR

Desiree L. Woods is a Christian writer, Detroit-native with southern roots, entrepreneur, and mentor. She is inspired to write books to help people struggling with issues as further described. She uses her ability to capture the core of the problems and provide comfort, hope and resources. She is the author behind this book Part One of a Trilogy: 'Tina Unexpected Pleasures, Unanticipated Pain: Addressed to Teen Moms & their Families; and Part Two 'GEM: A Positive Commute Ending Domestic Violence'; Part III 'Wormhole-Imbroglio to Disengage-Freedom from Substance Abuse'. She is also the author of 'You Can Say That-The Doors We Close', to help you recognize the signs of inappropriate behaviors and to comfort those struggling with sexual trauma in hope of getting past the distresses. She has experienced sexual trauma, been a Teen Mom; Escaped Domestic Violence and had a bout with Substance Abuse, and now is victorious over all those areas, and desires to help others transition triumphantly.

DEDICATION PAGE

This book is dedicated to all the Teen Moms that are striving to cross the finish line with no regrets! To the families of the teens; to the new parent, those just starting - keep pushing, it gets easier! Some outcomes are not as we planned it to be; some relationships are not as we expected them to be; and some acquaintances are far better than we ever imagined! There are some outcomes that are totally out of our hand, understand the spirit that is operating and move forward. It's possible you may experience all the above simultaneously.

Win Some, Lose Some…Be Encouraged!

TINA
Unexpected Pleasure, Unanticipated Pain

This book is to give reassurance to the Teenage Mothers and the families of the Teen Moms. This book is also to help those that must reach outside the family for support.

There are different situations that lead up to becoming a Teen Mother and because a certain stigma-shame or disgrace, is associated with being a teen mom: I want the teen to know that "You can rise above the stigma, you are not an oversight, you can make it".

Understand family members of the teen, your interaction with them both is so very much important for all of you. We all can agree, the child is innocent, didn't plan to be here, didn't have an agenda and will except you and all the love you have to give. Isn't that a good place to make an invest? Support comes in many ways and forms. Mental, emotional, physical, and financial. Just pick one or two means that you can be supportive?

TINA
Unexpected Pleasure, Unanticipated Pain

Below are a few Famous Teen Moms:

Anna Nicole Smith

Aretha Franklin

Bristol Palin

Fantasia Barrino

Jamie Lynn Spears

Keisha Castle- Hughes

Loretta Lynn

Maya Angelou

Roseanne Barr

Sofia Vergara

Solange Knowles

Susan Somers

Whoopi Goldberg

TINA - ABSTRACTIONS & HINDSIGHT

INTRODUCTION

Abstractions- *the quality of dealing with ideas rather than results: it 'displays' only the relevant attributes, and it 'hides' the unnecessary or necessary details*

Hindsight *- understanding of a situation or event only after it has happened or developed.*

Webster Dictionary

INTRODUCTION

Teen Girls are full of ideas, and depending on where they are centered, determines their focus. They don't fit where they sprouted from and don't quite fit where they are growing too. If a teen has positive directions as far as education, surrounded by peers of the same magnitude, with optimistic role models, social and recreational outlets, that's good. That may decrease the numbers on a preventive scale; but you must also take into consideration: Sex Education; absent hours of constructive adult presence; social media exposure; inappropriate behaviors between an adult and teenager; and peer pressure. Covering all that still leaves a 2% chance of the unexpected…the teens own will power.

The Gamut is very wide as to why there are so many teenage mothers in all social economic levels. I don't want to go into how it happened. However, some teens may need counseling in that area because of a traumatic situation, and it is important in that aspect to do so; but this book is to help you pick up the pieces and move forward with determination,

INTRODUCTION

to help you be the best mother and individual you can be. This book is not meant to point the finger and find fault in the Teen Mom or the parents, but to help them in their growth and bridge the gap in family relationships if possible. If the relationship has unreconcilable differences then grab the support and connections that are mentioned here and move forward. Forgive and forget! There are some cases where the lack of money is not an obstacle in that case, support comes in more ways than financial. Emotional support is just as important and needed. There are some relationships that cannot be mended; so sad to say life goes on. What it all boils down to is: being a family is determined more by conduct than by blood. This book is meant to provide support and highlight objectives. I discovered that the breakdown most of the time was not in a discouraged Teen Mom but in the gap between family members. I hope to give you what's necessary to bridge that gap, mend relations and provide support.

TINA- UNEXPECTED PLEASURES & UNANTICAPATED PAIN
INTRODUCTION

Sometimes just saying, "Good job!" is enough. There are some relationships that will take time to mend. In the meantime, life goes on. There are outside services, mentors, therapist churches and organizations that can fill in the gap when family is unavailable, for whatever reason.

This book is to shed some light on parenting but basically to connect you to the resources and for you to know you are not alone: to help those that have given birth, and to tear down the stigma and humiliation that comes with it. Also, to assist Teen Moms in being successful. To shed light on the subject, so that the families can realize the importance of relationships.

HINDSIGHT

My pastor's wife asked me this question, "What would you say to your younger self?". I would say to my younger self, follow your dreams. Don't let anyone or anything deter you from that. Everybody has an emergency they feel is more important than what your goals and ambitions are. It is okay to say, "No, I apologize, I am unavailable" or "I appreciate that but", stay focused! Get your education first is easier. "But the other alternative is that you may be good at hair and make-up, cooking or baking, designing & sewing, or other creative entities that could pan out lucrative. Hindsight-Make a plan and Stay Focused". Travel, yes broaden your horizon, see the world then you'll know better what route to choose. Then settle down. You won't have any should've, would've, could've. Now that is the ideal way to do it. But for those that happened to become a Teen Mom, this book is to push your creativity to be your better self and use alternative methods that are at your disposal. You can still get your education, travel and settle down, you just have another soul to include in the plan.

THE OBJECTIVE OF THIS BOOK

This book is written with a foundation of theological precepts, inspirational affirmations known to affect you mentally, spiritually, and emotionally. To help you in day-to-day situations.

Also included are steps from known resources such as therapeutic and medical to balance us when those components are out of whack.

As well as the physical and social service resources for Mentors, Housing, Education and Employment purposes.

We know partnerships are important because one person cannot do it all. (It takes more than mom & dad to raise a child.) Therefore, we have referrals and resources from Social Service entities, clinical agencies for mental and physical health, nonprofit agencies and brick and mortar corporations to assist with basic needs, financial management and revenues.

OVERCOMING STARES AND COMMENTS

There are two types of stares and comments. Those that say, "You are the perfect picture of Motherhood"; "You take such good care of your baby". "You make mothering look easy, my God you don't even yell at your children!". These types of comments encourage you and confirm that you are on the right track.

On the other hand, those that comment, "She look like a baby herself"; "I can't tell the child from the mother" or whisper, "ugh, ugh, ugh".

> Just pray that God remove that judgmental spirit off of them: and say in your mind, *"If I weren't old enough then it could not have happened! Be at Peace... Moving Forward!*

OVERCOMING STARES AND COMMENTS

In Memory of Those That Moved to Heaven

My Son, My Daughter,

My Love

My Sweet

Little Boy, Little Girl.

I would give

The world and

Me in it for

You to live painlessly,

I would give you my Lung

To allow you to breath,

I would give you my bowel

It would allow you to feed.

My love for you goes deep.

I only wish for you to arise

from pain and sickness.

To hold you free from tubes and lines.

Memory of Those That Moved to Heaven

You see… to watch you crawl on
your knees, to hear your first
words recorded in history…
I only hope for peace with you
I hope I'm not pushing you to
do something you don't want,
but it's only because I love you.
No more tears, no more fears
The Lord has arrived to answer
my cry. Not a mistake HE came
To take you away. I miss you always
I love you no less these days
I'm sad but happy you're free
No more doctors and nurses in
Your face.

Memory of Those That Moved to Heaven

Goodbye my love is what
I need to say, we all know
Heaven is the best place.
Say hello to Jesus and save me
a space. Goodnight my sweet
Rest in Peace!

by Maria Denise

TO THE FAMILY

Have a positive mindset. It happened. Where do we go from here. This is a nephew or niece, grandchild, or cousin; an innocent being that had nothing to do with their entrance into this world. No thoughts or plans to be here. What we can do is make this transition a pleasant one? What can we do so that he or she won't experience schisms. That is divisions and separations between grandparent and mother, discord between siblings and straight up disharmony amongst the family. Sure, you had hopes it wouldn't go that way, but it did. You had plans it would go your way, but it didn't. We must put should've, would've, could've aside and apply Mercy and Grace. Think about it this way. A soul of innocence that will except all the help, guidance and love you can give them;

TO THE FAMILY

and maybe this person will grow up to be an inventor, entrepreneur, teacher or president. Or even a great sports player, entertainer or motivational speaker. The outcomes are endless and how you play a role in this child's life will level the playing field or break the advantages. What do you want to be known as? One that was supportive or one that…well, you fill in the blank. It really does take all hands-on deck!

DON'T GIVE UP ON YOUR DREAMS

If it is at all possible try to mend relations with your family. If not possible, move on forgive and forget. Ok so you're a Teen Mom now. Do I finish school. Yes of course. Whether it is to stay in Public or Private school or go to a specific school for pregnant girls & teen moms: or Adult Education or community college or a university; whatever, start with that. If it's college or trade school start with something. There are programs to assist with day care so that you can get your education. If there is no or little family support you may have to depend on organization that are set aside to help Teen Mothers or depend on Financial Aid or scholarships: this is a stepping stone.

You are beginning a family of your own, and there is help for your situations. Use it as a steppingstone. Remember steppingstones are just that, step by step, here a little there a little, until you reach your goal.

DON'T GIVE UP ON YOUR DREAMS

You may have a talent - Sewing, Cosmetology, Hair Broidery, Baking, Cooking, motivational speaking. Get the license, a business plan, a grant, or investor, a Go Fund Me account. Build up your clientele. Work at home until you can go into a shop or Brick & Mortar. Just don't give up on your dreams.

Unexpected Pleasures, Unanticipated Pain

Shoot yea! The labor was hard three days but afterwards the joy of a baby boy! I forgot all about the travail. Yes, I did experience Post-Partum Blues! I looked at the creature that demanded food, diaper changes and to be washed up at whatever time he deemed…1:30, 3:30 or 5:30 am it didn't matter. So, I spanked him on his little leg and he whimper this little cat sound. I saw he was helpless and immediately fell in love with him. Yea and I made sure he was fed, dry and clean. After a while there were longer intervals in-between, I got some sleep!

I have interviewed many teen moms and observed their interactions with their babies, and I saw a mother proud, a mother willing and a mother not scorned. Sacrificing for her child with patience; taking advantage of all the necessary resources, finishing school, and pursuing a career.

Unexpected Pleasures, Unanticipated Pain

Yes, most of the ones doing that had a good support team and some were not necessarily family. It was not always help from their mother, brothers and sisters or the father, but friends and extended family members, social services resources or the family of the daddy. Some of these Teens had mothers, sisters and aunties that stepped in. Thanks be to God! Most of the Teen Mom's I talked to said, when they were going through, they were very much encouraged and determined to be successful.

Win Some, Lose Some – Friends

So, let's talk about friends. You had some friends you cut your finger and mixed the blood and said, "friends forever": and as soon as you got pregnant, you didn't see them anymore, just in passing then puff! They were gone.

So, you make new friends, at the doctor's office or at your new school or in the park. By the way you don't have the same mindset to do the same kooky things you use to do.

You must get home or pick up baby from sitter and care for the child, and that's alright because you get pleasure out of that. So-what if those friends don't know by now, what they missed; they maybe could have been a God-parent they're loss.

Win Some, Lose Some – Friends

Also appoint someone as Godparent. Someone that you noticed that cares and want to pour into your child's life. You'll know them when you see them because they will be interested and loving. It's ok to have more than one Godparent.

It's important to have a support group. I didn't get lonely because I chose associates that had children and talked to adults that had wisdom. It would be difficult to do this by yourself. So say, 'see ya' to the old friends and hello to the new. Win some new and improved relationships and goodbye to the old acquaintances that would discourage you. Two of my friends had a sister that was in the Marvelettes. She and her Husband took me in and mentored me until I was able to go on my own. I am forever grateful for them. Her name was Annette (McMillan) her married name.

WIN SOME, LOSE SOME – FRIENDS

We know that all things work together for the good to them that love God… Romans 8:28

28

FAMILY
OVERCOMING WHAT PEOPLE SAY

What will people say to you supporting your family. What will people say to you affecting a life in a positive Manner. Does it really matter? People will talk whether you do good or bad. So, if you are involved doing what you can, to fill in the gap such as babysitting, supplying a need, saying an encouraging word, providing transportation or helping with housing: the outcomes will be amazing!

Life is too short to be concerned about what a person thinks or will say, especially if they are not in your inner circle. If they are in your inner circle and not inspirational, it's time to let them go. If it is a stranger passing by, how much authority over your life do you give someone you may never see again in life?

FAMILY
OVERCOMING WHAT PEOPLE SAY

What matters is that you can make a positive effect in the life of a child or family member. Do unto others as you would have them do unto you. What you do for others will come back on you. You never know if that very child might be the one you have to count on later in life.

Don't look back at the disappointment or failed dreams. Look ahead make new dreams, pick up the pieces, move forward!

If you are already motivated and moving forward – Good Job! Give this book to someone you think might need it! Pass it forward!

FAMILY
OVERCOMING WHAT PEOPLE SAY

Later in life I was the one that had to bathe my mother, make sure she was getting quality health care services and have people that would take care for her around the clock and yes funeral arrangements. See how God turned the tables around.

TRUSTING THE PROCESS

Teens if you set a plan for Education, stick to it. The outcome will be beneficial in finding a position or career path that will sustain you. It can be attending a professional trade school or higher education; a strategic plan to build and grow a business.

You must trust the process. There is 'seed time and harvest', cause and effect. Your efforts will pay off when you put the time in.

It can be laborious but utilizing the things required to grow and become a prosperous, informed adult, as you prepare for your future, will reap great outcomes. **Parents of the teen**, all we can do as a parent is present the good and warn of the evil & teach survival and knowing your triggers; and most of all trust in God.

TRUSTING THE PROCESS

Our part is to provide the essential keys for growth & maturity. Sometimes just being supportive will go a long way.

As an individual, a teen, you have the capacity to think for yourself and choose good or bad:
with that being said, you are liable for our own actions.

You as a parent, can hope that a child chooses the right direction. Your hands are clean. That means You don't have to account for their actions, it's on them. If you've done what is required of you as a parent; then you are freed from penalties and can share in the outcomes of guiltless; good planning and a boundless optimistic conclusion.

Teen Mom know that you have charge over a life at least for the next 21 years. Make the most of it and build precious memories.

OVERTURNED

For Those Who Come from Toxic Environments

Now there are situations that are not perfect. Maybe you came from a house with a single parent that was on drugs or an alcoholic; or come from some kind of abuse-mental, emotional or physical: maybe it is a non-supportive attitude of a parent or caregiver: or a so called, "idea home", where one or both parents are just zero tolerant toward teen pregnancy.

Whatever the scenario, if we are under it, it can affect us. Just know that no abuse, manipulations, or intolerance, dictates who you are or your destiny.

We can overcome all obstacles! First of all,
if it's necessary, go to a Safe House.
Call 211 for help and resources such as

OVERTURNED

Programs for Teen Moms, Teen Pregnancy Housing, Teen Moms for Homeless or Battered Teen Programs or call '988' for Mental Health Assistance.

Resources are available for whatever your need to escape the abuse or neglect.

Don't be afraid to ask for help. We can also look for help at a local church, or Social Service organizations, a friend or relative. There are helpful agencies listed in the back of this book.

Also, in applying the word of God we can make positive declarations and act on them. If we need to talk to someone we trust or a therapist, do so. If we need medical attention get it. Surround yourself with positive people and have a plan in place. Get a strategy to rise above your circumstances.

TINA
UNEXPECTED PLEASURE UNANTICIPATED PAIN
AFFIRMATIONS | DECLARATIONS

POSITIVE AFFIRMATIONS

I am successful, I am confident,

I am powerful, I am strong.

I am beautiful, I am focused.

I am getting better and better every day.

I wake up motivated.

I am an unstoppable force of nature.

I believe in my dreams.

I am doing my best every day.

I love myself for who God say I am

I take charge of my own happiness

I am walking in greatness!

I am walking in faith knowing my

Plans will come to pass.

I am the head and not the tail,

Above only and not beneath

POSITIVE AFFIRMATIONS

I can do all things in Christ which strengthens me.
Philippians 4:13

And we know that all things work together for good to them that love God, and are the called, according to his purpose. Romans 8:25

I am a child of the King; it would be worse for him that offend me that a millstone be tied around his neck and he be tossed into the sea… then to mess with one of His. Matthew 18:6

I am who God says I am, I can do what God says I can do, I am more than a conqueror, Romans 8:37

I am fearfully and wonderfully made. Psalms 139:14

I'm blessed when I go in and blessed when I come out. Deuteronomy 28:6

POSITIVE AFFIRMATIONS

He will give me beauty for ashes,

The oil of joy for mourning

The garment of praise for the spirit of heaviness

That I might be called the tree of righteousness

The rooted in the Lord

That he might be glorified. Isiah 61:3

I can arise above my circumstances.

My help comes from the Lord! Psalm 121:2

POSITIVE AFFIRMATIONS

I thank God for every day
Forgetting those things that are behind and
Reaching forward to the things ahead…Philippians 3:13

I am persuaded, that neither death, nor life, nor angels, nor principalities, nor powers, nor things present, nor things to come, nor height, nor depth, nor any other creature, shall be able to separate me from the love of God which is in Christ Jesus. Romans 8:38-39

POSITIVE AFFIRMATIONS

Blessed are the poor in spirit:
for theirs is the Kingdom of God
Blessed are they that mourn:
for they shall be comforted
Blessed are the meek:
for they shall inherit the earth
Blessed are they which do hunger and thirst after
righteousness: for they shall be filled
Blessed are the merciful:
for they shall obtain mercy
Blessed are the pure in heart
for they shall see God
Blessed are the peacemakers:
for they shall be called the children of God
Blessed are they which are persecuted
for righteousness' sake;
for theirs is the kingdom of heaven
Blessed are you, when men shall revile you,

POSITIVE AFFIRMATIONS

and persecute you, and shall say all manner of evil against you falsely, Rejoice, and be exceeding glad; for great is your reward ... Matthew 5:3-12

ABSTRACTIONS
I Suppose I'll Have a Baby!

14 years old, this is how I see it...
Can I get some love, Mother?
Isn't that what Moms are for?
To look out for her child,
To encourage her,
To shield and protect.
Have good times together,
and get through the bad moments,
To have an awesome relationship with,
That nobody can separate?

I know you should have my back - see no evil,
think no evil, do know evil, love never fails;
Believe all things, endure all things, hope…

Well… since you find that a little hard to do,
I think I'll show you how it's done.

I'll have somebody to love… *and* love me back
I will give UNCONDITIONAL LOVE, that
Nobody can break the bond or steal away:

ABSTRACTIONS
I Suppose I'll Have a Baby

I see. Since I'm accused of doing 'it' I
might as well... I can do this. /well
I wash, cook, clean, shop and pay
the bills...why not?
This road I walk will be just me and my baby... I
suppose I'll Have a Baby!

by D.L. Woods

okay, we know this is Stinking Thinking! Just in case you are feeling this way! The thing to do in this situation is to be the best you can be. Prove them wrong! God can love you like nobody else could! I dare you to try Him! He will turn your darkness into light, make your load lighter. He'll be a Battle Axe! Make your enemies be at peace with you, and bless you No Doubt!

REFERENCES TO TITLE

The meaning of Tina: Follower of Christ
            in Latin- She who follows Christ
Unexpected Pleasures - Sometimes the pleasures is wonderful but can turn into Unexpected Pain. With the exception of being raped, all things leading up to conception I am pretty sure was quite pleasurable. The gifts, impromptu fun and happy occasions, the winning and dining; the poetic moments, the making love, need I say any more.

The unanticipated pain- let's start with delivering a child, sleepless nights, a lifestyle change. When your brother or sister throw hard words at you; your friends turn their back on you; your Mama or Daddy kick you out the house; your Auntie or Uncle give up on you— that's unanticipated pain.

Let that pain make you stronger. Make them out of a liar! Set your face like flint so that it burns up every bad word and not dwell in your heart. When it comes to your mind, reject it don't dwell on it. The bad deeds that were done you put it under your feet and let it take you higher. The lies they tell, laugh at it! Don't let it hold you hostage! Stay focused so when rejection comes, put it under your feet and keep it moving!

ABSTRACTIONS AND HINDSIGHT

Abstraction- the quality of dealing with ideas
           than event or outcomes.
For example: "I think I'll have a baby". That statement without considering it's a life changing event, the cost to raise a child, childcare, housing, education, finance, the father and the fact that the baby is going to grow up. Abstraction! You have to consider all things that it would entail to get to a certain goal or not to take that road at all.

Hindsight- Understanding of a situation or event
           only after it has happened or developed.

Hindsight is where you develop the wisdom after the fact. Wouldn't you much rather listen and learn or follow a path where you know what the outcomes will be? Although hindsight is good for development and changing direction.

TINA
Unexpected Pleasures, Unanticipated Pain
ANTHOLOGY

Unexpected Pleasures, Unanticipated Pain

For those that don't have a perfect mother

I FORGIVE YOU MOTHER

I Forgive you
The Lord erased every hurtful thing
you did to me; I still love you
But I've moved on

I forgive you for not supporting me,
Restraining me, reframing me
for your benefit.

Yes, Oh Queen
Under your control, I
lived at your beckon call,
and spent a lot of time in my room.
My friends were my books.
So, I stayed at home-
washing clothes, and cleaning up.

Unexpected Pleasures, Unanticipated Pain

For those that don't have a perfect mother

I FORGIVE YOU MOTHER

My out time was grocery shopping,
Paying bills, picking up prescriptions.
Your reasoning was, "this is what girls do"
(you don't!)

I asked why they get to go! You said,
"I'm a girl I can't go by myself"
How you pretended to be concerned.

But I'll give it to you-
You made up for it by taking me shopping:
I could pick out whatever I wanted,
Gold or silver earrings and the price tag
on the cloths did not matter…once a season
this pleasure you afforded me.
Other times you wished I was
turned out in the streets.

I FORGIVE YOU MOTHER

As a young adult…I had my days of depression, especially on Christmas…Why? Because the world shut down on that day. I could not have happiness in outside pleasures! This day was centered around family!

I could not be alone and expect the enjoyment from TV because what was on the screen was centered around death, suicide, depression or Christmas Joy. But now, since my joy is inward springing out and I have forgiven you. I have forgiven me also; the joy of the Lord is my strength! I'm moving forward

I ask this question one last time
What mother would hate her child,
Try to turn her children against her, when pretending to take care of them…you cared for your pick, the others you turned to the state while playing the loving grandmother.

I FORGIVE YOU MOTHER

What mother would go out of her way to make her daughter's life miserable and at the same time call other females' daughter. If they saw what that word meant to me, they wouldn't want to be called that!
So, I've Released! All pain, hurt, questions, tears and fears with this consolation:

Christ said, *he set a man at Variance against his father and the daughter against her mother and the daughter in law against her mother-in-law and a man's foe shall be they of his own household.*
He that loves father or mother more than me is not worthy of me and he that loves son or daughter more than me is not worthy of me and he that takes not his cross, and follows after me, is not worthy of me.
Matthew 10:35-38

That Passage Made Me Strong
I wiped my tears!

I FORGIVE YOU MOTHER

Gave up my fears, it made me a winner,
it made me a survivor, more than a conqueror!
I found my worth in the Fathers' love,
so yes, I forgive you. The pain, hurt,
shame, tears and fears dissipated.
Satan negated! HE gave his only Son that I might
live abundantly and have everlasting Love!
So, think it not strange that you are not in the perfect
family - You are not alone, and God can bring good
even out of this! My decision to move on is solid and
I except the Gift of God and have moved forward!
Rest in Peace, Oh-Queen.

Unexpected Pleasures, Unanticipated Pain
COMMENTARY

As a child I looked at my mother as being a strong independent woman, that didn't take no mess. She taught me to be a strong, independent woman and don't take no mess! I didn't find out until I was much older, when I sent my 16-year-old son to stay with her, after he wouldn't abide by my rules; skipping school sneaking out the house late: I knew she would show him a thing or two; but she didn't. She was only that way with me. She spoiled him gave him everything and he was also able to manipulate her.

I loved my mother until her death. I went to her church a couple weeks after her death. When I got there the praise team was singing and I was rejoicing with them. Then they stopped singing. It was only a rehearsal before church. So, I sat down and I looked at the seat in the front where she usually sits. She wasn't there. And I looked all around for the pastor and his wife and didn't see them. Grief hit me-it knocked me off my square! I said in my mind I better get

COMMENTARY

up and get out of here. If I can just make it to the car. I made it to the car I began to lose it. I cried uncontrollably snot and tears running everywhere, I couldn't hardly catch my breath and a missionary knocked on the window like the police and asked what's the matter, is there anything I can do for you or the pastor can do for you? And I'm trying to talk and was stuttering, I just buried my mother, this her church and the tears and the snot is flowing uncontrollably and she said, "PEACE BE STILL!" and immediately I felt a calm, it was like the Lord himself had me in his arms! I calmed down and was able to go back into the church and stay until the end. I don't know if I would recognize that woman-that angel again but I thank God for her!

I never would have thought that I would have reacted in that manner. I was cool from the time I had to view her body in the hospital before they took her away. Through the awake the funeral home, picking out the casket to the repass and

COMMENTARY

through her things and distributing them. I didn't feel a thing. I was totally out of character! I asked God why did I react in that manner and He said, "Because you sincerely loved her"; and I did. I could not change the way she felt about me but I loved her just as if she did.

Grief can strike at any time and any place. When it does it takes the spirit of God to bring comfort.

Her mother, my grandmother told me when I was 14 years old that she was incapable of giving me love, so don't hate her; and I didn't. When I was able to except her as she is (that took the Holy Spirit and the Word of God), she couldn't hurt me anymore! She still did things and tried to hurt me up unto her death. I stayed in my lane. I understood the spirit that was in operation. I learned how I could be around her and when to fold. There were no hard feelings. I was only able to forgive her because of my place in God. This is just one of the relationships that are not as we expect them to be. Forgiveness is for ourself. Forgive and move forward!

TINA
Unexpected Pleasures, Unanticipated Pain
HOUSING PROGRAMS FOR TEEN MOMS

HOUSING PROGRAMS FOR TEEN MOMS

This book has anecdotes and insight on real life experiences and commitments. Also included are resources to help you mentally, spiritually, your physical wellbeing and circumstances. Help can come in many aspects. Perhaps I can shorten your time spent looking for the resources needed and point you in the right direction. The end game is, improve the quality of your life.

It would take a very thick book to add all the resources form every city and state. If yours is not listed, google 'Housing Programs for Teen Mom', 'Resources for Teen Moms', 'Non Profit Counseling for Teens', 'Companies that hire Teens', 'Education Programs for Teen': I think you got now.

Housing for Teen Moms

Bethlehem House
Social services organization
5063 Van Dyke St
Open 24 hours
(313) 923-6435

Mom's Place II -
Cass Community
Non-profit organization
1464 Webb St · In Cass
Community Social Services
Open 24 hours
(313) 865-4022
http://casscommunity.org

Covenant House Michigan
Non-profit organization
2959 Martin Luther King Jr Blvd
Closed · Opens 9AM Mon ·
 (313) 463-2000
http://www.covenanthousemi.org

Alternatives For Girls
Social services organization
903 W Grand Blvd
Closed · Opens 9AM Mon ·
(313) 361-4000
https://alternativeforgirls.org
Their website mentions teen pregnancy

Detroit Rescue Mission Ministries
Genesis House 1
150 Stimson St
8:30AM Mon ·
(313) 993-4700
Their website
mentions teenage, parents, and homes
http://www.drmm.org

Teen Parent Services
1630 Gratiot Ave
Saginaw, MI 48602
Phone: (989) 792-6789
https://www.ypccares.org/supporting-educating-teen-parents

Housing for Teen Moms

Teen Parent Services
2806 Davenport
Saginaw, MI 48602
(989) 792-6789
https://www.ypccares.org/supporting-educating-teen-parents

Birthright of Macomb
8076 21 Mile RD
Shelby TWP 48317
586-254-5930
https://birthright.org

Housing for Teen Moms

Love N Kindness Transitional Housing
Assisted living facility
12249 Camden Ave
(313) 521-8304

Saras House/Place Store
20150 Monica St
Closed · Opens 8:30AM Mon
(313) 473-7814
https://www.sarashouse.org

Birthright of Macomb County
4.0(4) · Pregnancy care center
8076 21 Mile Rd
Shelby Twp, MI 48317
Opens 10AM Mon
586-254-5930

New Moms (Chicago)
5317 W. Chicago Ave
Chicago, Ill 60651
New Moms (Western Suburbs)
206 Chicago Ave
Oak Park, IL 60302
773-252-3253
773-252-5320
contact@newmoms.org

Saginaw County Youth Project
2806 Davenport Ave
Saginaw, MI 48602
989-755-0937
https://www.ypccares.org

Housing for Teen Moms

Mom's House
2505 Franklin Ave
Toledo, OH 43610
419-241-5554
www.Momshousetoledo.org
https://momshousetoledo.org

Housing for Teen Moms

Jessie's Non Profit Homes
1-416-365-1888
https://jessiecentre.org
mail@jessiecentre.org

Hearts and Homes
3919 National Drive Suit 400
Burtonsville, MD 20866
301-589-8444
Intake 443-610-9407
admissions@heartsandhomes.org

Housing for Teen Moms

Baltimore, MD
410-602-5313
https://heartsandhomes.org/teen-mothers

Mothers Helping Mothers
877-858-8890
614-383-8180
mhmoffice@mhmteen.org
P.O. Box 30181
Gahanna, Oh 43230
Columbus, OH

Child and Family Charities
4287 Five Oaks Drive
Lansing, MI 48911
517-882-4000
877-833-3689
Mon-Thurs 8:30-7pm
Friday 8:00- 5pm

Alternative House AYM
(Assisting Young Mothers)
Ages 18-22
P.O. Box 694
Dunn Loring, VA 22027-0000
Fairfax, VA
703-280-2162   TDD: 711
703-280-2163 Fax
Text '**TEENHELP**' to **85511**

Housing for Teen Moms
Second Story
www.Second-story.org/young-mothers
Ages 16-24
Crisis Hotline (Virginia Area)
866-654-8474
Text 'TEENHELP' to 85511

Methodist Children's House
26645 W. Six Mile Road,
Redford, MI 48240
313-531-4060
Redford Charter Twp, MI

Humewood House
1102 Broadview Ave
Toronto, Ontario M4K 2S5
info@massey.ca
416-425-6348 X230
416-425-4056 Fax
York, ON, Canada

Young Mothers of America
520 East Washington Blvd.
Fort Wayne, IN 46802
https://ymoafw.org
571-298-7618

Housing for Teen Moms

Young Mothers of America
Non-profit organization
Fort Wayne, IN · In Tree-Life Missionary Baptist
Opens 9AM Mon
(571) 298-7618
http://www.ymoafw.org
Housing for Teen Moms

Mom's House
Toledo, OH
Opens 6AM Mon
(419) 241-5554
https://momshousetoledo.org

St Ann's Center for Children, Youth & Families
Social services organization
Hyattsville, MD
Open 24 hours
301) 559-5500
http://www.stanns.org
Social services organization
Glen Ellyn, IL
Opens 8:30AM Mon
(630) 790-8433
http://teenparentconnection.org
Housing for Teen Moms

The Center for Youth
Youth Social Services Organization
Rochester, NY
Opens 8AM Mon ·
(585) 271-7670
http://www.centerforyouth.net

Genesis House
Non-profit organization
Pittsburgh, PA
Open 24 hours · (412) 766-2693
https://genesispgh.org/genesis-house

Almost Home
Women's organization
St. Louis, MO
(314) 771-4663
http://almosthomestl.org

Jessie's - The June Callwood Centre for Young Women
Association or organization
Toronto, ON, Canada
Closed · Opens 9AM Mon ·
+1 416-365-1888

61

Dial "**211**" WNY
Non-profit organization
Buffalo, NY
(888) 696-9211
http://www.211wny.org

Grace's Table
Non-profit organization
Grand Rapids, MI
(616) 340-4309

New Beginnings -
A Home for Mothers
Association or organization
Milwaukee, WI
(800) 720-6667
https://homeformothers.com/newsletter.html
Teen Parent Connection

Life Haven
Non-profit organization
St Paul, MN
(651) 776-9805
www.lssmn.org

Monica Place School
Waterloo, ON, Canada
+1 519-743-0291
YWCA
Non-profit organization
Rochester, NY
(585) 546-5820
https://ywcarochester.org

Promise House Inc.
Non-profit organization
Dallas, TX
Open · Closes 12AM
(214) 941-8578

Good Shepherd Regina's Place
Youth center
Hamilton, ON, Canada
+1 905-549-4276
https://goodshepherdcentres.ca

Covenant House New York
Homeless shelter
460 West 41 Street
New York, NY 10036
Open 24 hours ·
 (212) 613-0300
https://ny.covenanthouse.org

House of Dawn Group home
Jonesboro, GA
Opens 9AM Mon ·
 (770) 477-2385
https://houseofdawn.org
houseofdawn1@bellsouth.net
PO Box 56
Richfield, WI 53076
1-800-720-MOMS (6667)

Housing for Teen Moms

Life Haven
Non-profit organization
St Paul, MN
(651) 776-9805
www.lssmn.org

Monica Place School
Waterloo, ON, Canada
+1 519-743-0291

Rosemary's Babies Co.
Non-profit organization
Cincinnati, OH
Closed · Opens 12AM Sun ·
(513) 813-8336
www.rosemarysbabies.co

YWCA
Non-profit organization
Rochester, NY
(585) 546-5820
https://ywcarochester.org

Promise House Inc.
Non-profit organization
Dallas, TX
Closes 12AM
(214) 941-8578

Good Shepherd Regina's Place
Hamilton, ON, Canada
+1 905-549-4276
https://goodshepherdcentres.ca

Covenant House New York
Homeless shelter
New York, NY
Open 24 hours ·
(212) 613-0300
Home - Covenant House NY

The Night Ministry
Social services organization
Chicago, IL
Opens 8AM Sun
(773) 784-9000

Mother-Child Residential Services
4.3(9) · Charity
Woodbury, NJ
(856) 853-1761
http://centerffs.org

Housing for Teen Moms

Rosalie Hall
Center for Family Services
Scarborough, ON, Canada
Opens 8:30AM
+1 416-438-6880
www.(centerffs.org)

Pregnancy care center
 714) 730-0930
https://www.maryspath.org
Viola's House
Association or organization
Dallas, TX
Closed · Opens 10AM Mon
(469) 751-2017
https://violashouse.org

The Northwest Center
Social services organization
Washington, DC
Opens 9:30AM Mon ·
(202) 483-7008
http://www.northwestcenter.org
The Lullaby House
Dallas, TX
Opens 9AM Mon
(469) 779-7076
https://www.lullabyhouses.com

 Mary's Path
18221 17th ST Santa
Ana, CA 92705

The Center for Healthy Families
Family counselor
Columbus, OH
Opens 12AM Mon ·
(614) 884-4200
http://centerforhealthyfamilies.org/
United Way of Central Ohio
Non-profit organization
Columbus, OH
 (614) 227-2700
https://liveunitedcentralohio.org

Hope House Colorado
Non-profit organization
Arvada, CO
Opens 8:30AM Mon
 (303) 429-1012
www.hopehousecolorado.org

Seton Home
Non-profit organization
San Antonio, TX
(210) 533-3504
https://setonhomesa.org

Counseling Resources for Teen Moms

Detroit Health Department
City government office
100 Mack Ave
Opens 8AM Mon ·
(313) 876-4000
Immunizations
313 876-4667
313-876-0133

Samaritan Counseling Center
Non-profit organization
Farmington Hills, MI ·
(248) 474-4701
Crossroads
Non-profit organization
Windsor, ON, Canada
Opens 9am
519-252-5456

Mind Wellness Counseling
Psychotherapist
Royal Oak, Michigan
123 S Main St Suite 100,
Royal Oak, MI 48067
Open · Closes 9PM
Appointment required
(248) 692-4013

Great Lakes
Psychology Group Counselor
Southgate, MI
734-215-9800

800-950-6264 **Hotline**
10am -10pm EST

TEXT **'NAMI'** to **'741741'**
Samaritan Counseling Center
Non-profit organization
Farmington Hills, MI
Closed · Opens 9AM
Wed · (248) 474-4701
Inwood House
Non-profit organization
New York, NY
https://childrensvillage.org/
(212) 742-2710

TEXT **'NAMI'** to **'741741'**
2900 Conner St Bldg. A
Detroit, MI 48215
namidetroit@gmail.com

Motor City Center for Hope
Counselor
18244 W McNichols Rd
 (313) 694-3886

Southwest Solutions
Non-profit organization
5716 Michigan Ave #3000
Closed · Opens 8:30AM
Wed · (313) 481-3102
Livonia, MI Open · Closes
8PM · (734) 331-0814

Counseling Resources for Teen Moms

Family Counseling & Shelter
Non-profit organization
Monroe, MI · In Harwood Plaza
(734) 241-0180

The Guidance Center
Non-profit organization
Allen Park, MI
Opens 9AM Wed · (734) 785-7700

Legacy Associates Foundation
No reviews · Non-profit organization
65 Cadillac Square Suite 2200 · In Cadillac Tower
(313) 309-3230

Abayomi
Community Development Corporation
Non-profit organization
24331 Eight Mile Rd
(313) 541-9828

Community Housing Network
Non-profit organization
196 N Rose St.#30
Mt Clemens, MI 48043
586-221-5900
(734) 419-7538

Family Crisis Center
of Washtenaw
2385 S Huron Pkwy #2n, Ann Arbor, MI 48104I
(734) 660-7059

The MI Counselor Group LLC
Mental health clinic
Hazel Park, MI
(248) 289-0619

Crossroads
Non-profit organization
Windsor, ON, Canada
+1 519-252-5456

iAMERICA Behavioral & Mental Health
19445 W Warren Ave,
Detroit, MI 48228
Opens 10AM
313-307-0088

Michigan Counseling Group
Mental health clinic
Warren, MI
(586) 510-4992

Counseling Resources for Teen Moms

Arab American & Chaldean Council

Non-profit organization
38219 Mound Rd #102,
Sterling Heights, MI 48310
(586) 939-5016

GreenPath Financial Wellness,
24333 Lahser Rd #6041,
Southfield, MI 48033
Southfield, MI
Credit counseling service
800-550-1961

GreenPath
2470 Collingwood St #106
Woodward Ave.
Detroit, MI 48201
Phone: (313) 961-1018
2111 Woodward Ave #906
(800) 550-1961

The Guidance Center
Non-profit organization
18805 Wick Road
Allen Park, MI 48101
734-785-7700

Dads and Moms of Michigan
7285 Orchard Lake Rd, West
Bloomfield MI, 48322
Country Club Dr & Telegraph Rd
(248) 559-3237
Non-profit organization

Detroit Health Department
100 Mack Ave
Opens 8AM Mon ·
(313) 876-4000
1313 876-4667
High Lead Level
313-876-0133

Hegira Programs Inc
Psychotherapy
8623 N. Wayne Road, Suite 123
Westland, Michigan 48185
Phone: (734) 367-0469
Fax: (734) 367-0791
Non-profit organization
Livonia, MI
(734) 721-0200
Supported Housing &
Employment
8623 N. Wayne Road, #220
Westland, Michigan 48185
(734) 427-
(734) 427-0608

Motor City Center for Hope
Counselor
18244 W McNichols Rd
(313) 694-3886

Foundations Counseling
No reviews · Counselor
20.0 mi · Livonia, MI
 (734) 331-0814

U-Snap-Bac
Non-profit organization
14901 E Warren Ave
(313) 640-1100

Counseling Resources for Teen Moms

Detroit 90/90
Non-profit organization
485 W Milwaukee Ave
(313) 887-1613

Abayomi Community Development Corporation
Non-profit organization
24331 Eight Mile Rd
(313) 541-9828

Community Housing Network
Non-profit
5505 Corporate Drive #300
Troy, MI 48098
248-928-0111
248-928-0122 Fax

A Better Tomorrow Counseling Services, LLC
25245 Five Mile Rd
STE 500
Redford, MI 48239
(313) 395-0380
Call Kendra Sibert
Additional Location

A Better Tomorrow Counseling Services, LLC
23077 Greenfield Rd #260
Southfield, MI 48075
(248) 281-3862

Supporting Hands Counseling Services
Clinical Social Work/Therapist, LMSW

Verified by Psychology Today
Eastpointe, MI 48021
Call **Ebony Payns**
(313) 631-1504

Employment Options for Teens

https://www.michigan.gov/fyit/employment/job-options-for-teens

These are suggestions but we encourage you to use these resources as a steppingstone. To invest in a plan, starting with your current situation to include: education, whether it's to graduate from high school, attend community college, university or trade school. If you have skills or talents that you can turn into a business, devise a strategic plan and be accountable. Think outside the box and much success!

Administrative Assistant

Assisted Living Facilities

Babysitting Services

Camp Counselor

Car-detailing Services

Carpenter Helper

Catering

Cleaning

Corporate Office

Counter Attendant

Daycare Assistant

Dispatcher

Dog Walker

Educational tutoring

Errand, Messenger Service

Factory Assembler

Fast Food Restaurants

Freelance

Gas Station Attendant

Grocery Bagger

Grocery Stores

Hostess

Hotel Resort

Jobs for Younger Teens

Machine Operator

Mail Clerk

Masonry Helper

Movie Theatre

Municipal Park & Recreation

Online Web Business

Parking Attendant

PC Tutor

Receptionist

Retail Outlets

Summer Camp

Swimming Instructor

Tutor

Urban Farm Worker

Veterinarian Assistant

Waiter/Waitress

Warehouse Person

Yard Maintenance

CONCLUSION

I hope that you have read these pages and received inspiration, motivation, understanding and have a mindset to thrive. That you aim high and let nothing get in your way of you reaching your goals. When discouragement comes, you shake it off and put it under your feet. When negativity comes you set your face like a flint and allow it to burn up so that it doesn't get into your heart. That you enjoy every minute of your life and when it gets difficult you say, "THIS IS A JOURNEY" and keep it moving! That you reward yourself in each accomplishment and when someone offend you, forgive them, and forget. Not to the point that you put yourself in that position again, but just so you can move forward! I prophesy that your best life is in front of you starting now! What hindered you before will no longer hold you hostage…Powerful Women of God!

It Never Was Hard!

References: King James Version Bible

　　　　　　Marriam Webster Dictionary

www.ingramcontent.com/pod-product-compliance
Lightning Source LLC
Chambersburg PA
CBHW011550070526
44585CB00023B/2538